KNOTTED GRIEF

Naveen Kishore

KNOTTED GRIEF

CODA

wearing a transparent shadow, the young widow waits
and waits

KASHMIRIYAT

1

uncaged
this long ailing night
left to die
like an aging raven
unused
to flying failing
its wings
mortified
this cagelessness
humiliating

2

smothered
flame of candle
crushed
between thumb
and forefinger

charred night

3

burst into flame
solitary flower immolate
your petals detonating
like suicide vests
making pale
the glitter
of the stars the sky
shredded raining fire
scorching an earth
already weary
of its own blood

take back
the night

4

shatter stillness

the night
on crutches

5

the sun
shrouded
in a cloak of night

refusing
point blank
to rise

6

bird stripped
of sight
seeking
refuge
in a sky
full
of bullet wounds

7

burnt
stumps

gather
the ashes scatter
the ashes

into the wind

8

breaking
the silence

death's soft whisper

9

ash coloured
the cobblestones

10

above my head
smoke from
a distant dream

a sky
in flames

11

voiceless scream
as leaves
drop

one
by one

12

stitched from clouds
soaked
in red
the sky
reluctant shroud

13

smeared grey
across the sky
its ash visage
darkened
by the death
of the sun

14

is this
or is this
the dream
I came home to?

dogs sniffing blood
on chinar leaves

15

watermelon heads
explode
every single day

16

elsewhere
in tiny heaps
discarded
ash

shrouds
in mourning

17

crumpled
sheet of light
in a room made vacant
made lonely made fiction
by what else
death
dappled shadow
white black white white
blurry motion windswept
ricochet across room
slamming headfirst
into the wall
also white
crumpling
into a shivering
daze on spinning floor
with a bang and
a crash
breath panting
for breath breathlessly
swallowing
gasping air gasping
for breath out of breath
eyes wide rolling over and
over before closing shutting
down clanging
like shutters ungreased
metal rusted with years

the light no longer white yellow
age yellow with age
hinges squeaking
for oil remembering
gaze fixed
on unseen further point
in the fog dense
remember leaves
losing sheen
at the moment of their passing
falling falling sheet floating
down light as light weightless
almost
crumpled shadow of light
in room emptied
of thought

all of it

18

in a fragile landscape
ash coloured
leaves
seeking refuge
from the fire

19

shiver death
in the cold
cold
light of the sun

20

streets
full of rage

stones
grappling with fists
willing
to bleed

21

their eyes shut tight
dead men learning
to dream

22

the children cycle madly
homewards
under a sky hurling
hailstones

23

charred
flame
of the candle

a dream in ashes

24

mirror
vast and silent
the oars precise
slice
its stillness

a different rhythm

that of gunfire
intermittent
echoes
ringing
ringing
in ears
made deaf
by a silence
intimate
with roadside graves

25

burnt
blackened forever
the night

26

all night long
the smell
of tyres
burning

27

forest
full of tree trunks
gutted

28

at sunrise
the women
hurrying
to bury the night

29

stab each hand
one by one

smash the clocks
underfoot
one by
one

30

across
a landscape of green
the fresh
fresh smell
of blood
spilling

31

crushed underfoot
leaves
daring to breathe

32

from the corner of my eye
a blur of grey

leaking fugitive

33

stripped
made naked
the bitterness
of shadows

34

scattered
beneath the stones
reams
and reams
of poetry

35

they bury shadows
here
every night
under a moon
known for its brazenness

36

widowed sky
lamenting
its own drowning

37

giant sieve
soaked
in its own blood

the sky
riddled

38

the keening of widows
muffled by the shadows

39

on some days
on most days
all that remains
is for the night to end

40

yesterday's words
like stale bread
posing as poetry

41

the blood-coloured flowers
continue
to bloom

42

the women silent
stones
watching refusing
to shroud their heads
shroud
their heads

43

a sky
unable
to shrug off
its greyness

44

there where
the shadows
huddle
in quiet whispers

the restlessness of
trees

45

elsewhere
the sound
of bare feet

running

46

anointed in their own blood
the shadows refusing
to weep

47

slice the vein
and let the poem bleed
all over the white
all over

48

bloodied fists
smash the night

49

cold wet street
stones
strewn under
a flickering lamplight
like freshly plucked flowers

50

low rumble
deep tumbril
from well of throat
the cry rising
thick like smoke
choking
on its own fire
burn
burn the devastated land
strewn with stumps
charred
as mighty trees
one by one by
one fall prey
to what?
what? was it
that caused this
blindness
blind blind
rage blinded
thought
suspended
impossible then
to extinguish
flames
sparked by
shadows
full

of faces trapped
in rooms full
of shadows
staring staring
blankly
at reflections
of flames
ricocheting off the walls
before collapsing
into a heap
of ash rotten
rotting from within
their hearts
so full
so full of anger

white
drained of blood
the landscape
waiting for winter
and snow

51

rage
into the night
solitary shadow

hide
hide your shame

52

strangling silence

the night
sandpapers
its leaves
singing hoarse
its songs out of tune
broken voiced
wrangling
like bent reeds underwater
snarled in discord

the distant sighing
of the flute wind
whispering rustling
in harmony
faint

soft
shrill piercing
the sound of a car horn

persistent loud
lament

strangling

silence

53

assisted by hands gripped
firmly around its neck
pushing down
splashing wildly
the darkness

drowned

once and for all
into the pool of light

54

doors being slammed
street after street
eyelids shutting down
as the light retreated
slinking away on silent feet

leaving behind the debris
of crumbling shadows

55

the shadows peel
from the old ceiling
like plaster

as the red-faced chinar
stands helpless
its sap draining from wasted limbs

the distance between the horizon
and the back of my palm
measured by the flight of the bird with white wings

captive moth
on its back the weight of dying embers
ferried to and fro

elsewhere the echoes
of a candle flame muffled
by fingers that knew no pain

the stone floor
beginning to feel the cold
as bare footsteps walked over its grave

like a whisper
the angel gliding past
its silhouette fighting shy of the firelight

on a clear and blue sky is heard
the song of the winter wind
utterly and completely silent

a child's memory of the future?

56

gritty
the morning air
obstructed by a haze of ash
shut eyes racing
through unfinished dreams
of yesterday's duststorm
the sun blindfolded
stumbling past rays
stealing
the breath
out of a sky
rusted
choking on its own bile

57

they tried him
without a trial accusing
him of things he had not done
pronouncing guilt sentencing
as punishment they tied him
up wrapping a rope around him
arms parallel to his body
his wings like tightly clenched fists
bound to his arms as he stood proud and tall
shot him with a water cannon at 40 degrees below zero

frozen thus they lowered him
from the trapdoor in the sky
and cut the rope

the angel expelled

58

the silence at the centre of the forest
deafening

59

unannounced visitor
I dropped by into my dream
careful not to awaken the buried whispers
I lit a candle by their grave
startling the slumbering shadows into a frenzy of activity
bats taking wing flying blindly into each other
this in turn caused the whispers to awaken
look me in the eye
and begin to do what they did best

bear witness

60

on the pavement
lay shattered like a dream
unconcealed unrestrained
anger

against everything

61

rain drenched light
unraveled

clouds lost in a sky
no longer blue

grey blackened
the night

lowered its head
shame in shame

62

cold grey
the morning
hurrying
to bury the night

63

the heart of the city
a cemetery

of grief

64

trapped
silence
out of breath

65

nobody sings
any longer no
not even
in this valley once
on song

except

except
the dead
the dead

humming
in whispers

about their dying

66

death

unashamed
her lips the shape of whispers

brazen red

67

crushed cold
against the mist
damp face distorted

a constant nagging
this acid rain

68

smell the burnt flesh
as they march

their metal boots
burying
the city

under
a frozen mass
of black ice

69

on both sides of the scream
a forced silence

70

trampled skies
beaten into submission
mercilessly

71

on a shadowless noon
the cawing of crows

72

after the last scream
has died down
only the shadows remain

parched this throat

73

imagine then
the melancholy of the wind
as the innocent flower
its petals exploding
flying like missiles
armed
for unwitting destruction

74

debris

of desolation

75

dark tree giant oak
your branches
drenched in tears

76

wrinkled departures
in a hand
littered with grief

77

leaves buried under
freshly dug earth
rustling

78

trapped
in a solitary cell
her light stolen
the shine
gone
out of her eyes
her tears
blackened
the shame
of being ravaged
the moon lay
looking up at the ceiling
widowed

79

snuffed by fingers
that put out the light

the once steadfast
and upright
candle flame
lowered its head
into the palm
of its hand

something
resembling a long night
returned
to haunt the skies

80

in her eyes
a receding sun
withdrawing

81

storm clouds
a wall
blocking the sun
the dawn
without mercy
strangling
the rain

82

an ashen wind
holding its breath
confused
the solitary eagle
unable to fly

83

voices made mute
break their vow of silence
barefoot women fleeing
an approaching tumbril

84

a magician cuts the body in half
bowing
spellbound audience applauding
with bloody hands

85

the drunken ghost
collapsing at his own funeral
unnoticed by mourners
lowering himself into the earth

86

blood red flowers
signaling
an early spring

soon it will be time
for children to come out
to play

87

eyes
that question
endlessly

88

in knee deep ash
sifting through
memories

of a rage
long burnt out

89

gathering their soft fists around stones
girls learning to aim
throw
throw
throw

90

the poet runs
from his own words
into the arms of a stray bullet

91

night straying
into the arms of a dirge
grieving

92

bullet-ridden trees
tangled
a heart full
of whispers

93

flame bearing
tongues
warm
the winter bitterness
sky filled with smoke

94

its silence
broken
by the sound of oars
the night
sliced

95

clouds
wrapped shrouds
earth
on fire

96

shadow of a dream of red
biting back the blood
I pluck at the scars
made word made poetry made dirge

97

a wounded earth
awaiting
the onslaught of winter
snow

98

shroud
drained of blood
like a land dyed
white

99

a stone-faced disease
quietly spreading
blindness

100

speech
made voiceless
made
death

101

restless
echoes
gasping for breath
seeking
forgiveness

102

bullets
exploding
like poems
on a page

103

in a forest
full of sobbing trees
birds longing
for their cages

104

like a wordfinder
a thesaurus blinded
by the dark
I could smell the smoke the stench charred
it was going to be a long night
one that would burn
ceaselessly endlessly incessantly
unceasingly interminably constantly
perpetually continually relentlessly

105

the tiles crash to the ground
one by one

the sound of running feet?

STREET FULL OF WIDOWS

across the barb-wire   bisecting
           the curfew
stand three women
           their bodies covered
           in black
   only the red   of the eyes
guides them
       to graveyards

covered in snow
       this month of August
foretelling
the bitter winter

watch the men run
           die
   streets full of widows

the deserted street
allows the child
to play hopscotch
she hops on one leg then
the other
muttering names
of missing friends
under her breath
the lake waters listen
in silence
no one speaks ill of the dead
here no one
speaks
tongue hidden deep in your throat
you swallow

at the end of the longest street
crouching shadows
awaiting transport

just when you think you have seen enough
the night explodes
and another day begins

there are no more white lilies in the valley

the moon seeks an anchor as it dives
          headlong   into the lake
the black waters refuse
                    to budge

so many lives   unlived

my body feels so light in death
they will need to chain it to the leg of the iron bed

go gather the flowers   for the wreaths
go   from door to door
          gathering
                    the sheets for shrouds

there is no time to grieve

missing friends
their breath frosting
the winter air

their eyes refusing to blink
for fear of blindness

this is a delicate matter
one that requires tact
and no betrayal of anxiety

everyone
between the ages of 8 and 15 has been taken away

the wisdom of fathers who stand at the edge of the lantern light engaging the shadows into a conversation about the children who have disappeared later when you were to ask me about what happened I would open my mouth and show you the sores on my tongue

the keening rises out of the fog
            gasping for air   shuffling
footsteps   echo the weight
            of a fading daylight
on cobblestoned streets

soon the body-bearers will emerge
            carrying their burden

the blurred shadow frozen in mid-sentence

SELECTED GRIEFS

That Sunday again

filling
its lungs   breath

from a flybuzzing-stifling
stifled
stifled
afternoon breath

wheezing-scream kettle
steam steam
whistles
a stolen farewell

rain taps
on window on door
having turned its back
on the light

that Sunday again

bitter
afterthought
of silence being-begged
to perform
miracles
veiled crystals
rolled
into balls
of haze-gaze
reflecting eyes
hooded
in disbelief
gone

gone

condemned-patch
of tangled earth
throwing a tantrum
underneath the window

difficult weeds

storm rust clouds
gather above
disturbed branches
of the mango tree

half-uttered scream

undecided
weathervane hesitating
rain-crows foreseeing
an early grave

looking the other way

she
sat in silence
year after
year

mourning her own passing

where will you be this summer?

wind-mother

when the temperatures rise
like memory
and the train tracks   refuse

the haze   diminishes
the distance of not arriving nor
getting there   where
the mirror glints there
where the one
doesn't greet   the other

there

where the   haze diminishes where
the one doesn't meet the other
nor the distance of not arriving
nor getting there where
the mirror glints   there where

to hell with it I will write you a letter and post it

flower ironed hard between poems
printed on paper coarse-gray as rain
she remembered things
as diverse as overflowing sewage
and the musk of Japanese dolls
entrapped in glass-cases
on top of shelves that stared down
on whatelse
the dining table
hands press-squeezed
folded in rusted hope
and in her fist full of light
the dark sits sipping coffee

put down
everything
lists make *lists*
secure
in the sudden knowledge
of your leave *leavetaking*?
one that you
cannot
possibly
have known
or foreseen and
yet
you did know
foresee
did you not?
failing *failing* gently
to mention even
in passing
close as we were
companion of our almost summer
you left enough
crumbs for me
to unfold shadow
aftershadow carefully
stored hidden neatly
neatly hinting of
a time later
later when
I would need
need
to find my way home
it being no mean achievement

there was no sign of rain that morning
none
in fact it was business as usual
wake up turn to your husband request your tea collapse into his almost arms

and to think she had no practice

and that's the thing you see
it was unrehearsed
her departure

full
of paper cuts
fingers
flip the poems flick
yellowed pages
rustle up speed
freshly pressed
petals edging
out lost sheen
of older dried brittle
flowers
delicate inhabitants
of pages previously flipped
flicked
folded gathering dust
and silver fish

intrude
intrude
unsteady fog
the autumn leaves
have only just
        begun to fall

forgive me my shy grief

flame

waver
hesitate

burn

between the black
and the black lies
an abandoned shaft of light
floor wood-planked shuffle feet nervous
enter the stage lines mid-streaming
everything stops on cue before starting
split-second moment
startled beginning anew
the song
the story
the tale
lore
saga
opening wounds long forbidden
as eyes easy targets
beam crisscrossing stage
made thunder made storm
made taut
eyes follow
eyes as you rivet
nail the attention of an entire
audience enthralled
silently watching
every move you make words
you utter
you enunciate
you emote
enact make visible
the consummate actor that you are
Aren't you?

words fill my breath
less mouth with

breath leaving
          holes in our conversation
          causing

me to question   what

could possibly be happening
          for something is

I look around   unable

          to recognise   people around me
causing me to question
what could   possibly be causing breath   less mouth
to take breath
          words fail to register
inaudible
amongst   babble
being uttered
on the edge of language

failing steadfastly
          resolutely   refusing to
communicate   words

fill my mouth with   breath less ness
causing me to question   what
could possibly be happening

for something is
        I look around   unable

the rain its sameness
                        same
darkened puzzle
        unraveled
despair
unrivaled in its
sameness   same
        despair unravelling
puzzle its darkness
unrivaled
its   sameness
no longer a puzzle
the rain

        drowning

in despair   unrivaled

as things
in frustration

and
in sameness   unravel

sameness
sameness
same   puzzle

braided silence
learning to live
with knotted   grief
you do your own thing
when   you sing the grieving yes
you do your own thing   when you do
sing your grieving
knotted silence
braided grief
yes
you do learn to do your own thing
knotted braids grieving
silence knotted braids grieving
silence

hear it yourself first
            slowly then   in rhythm with
your own silence
braided grief you learn to
chase your gods into a corner
hide their light
plunge into darkness
tie them up
in knotted grief braided
silence

‘Stage the blues’ she said
to no one in particular and
much to her delight
I imagine
the stage she had strayed on to
in that vast and empty auditorium
turned a shade of silvery blue
as she kicked off her bebop-rebop sandals
flung backpack wing-wards and
humtum-shumtoed her way swiftly
like a modernday ballerina
dancing the emptiness
the timetapper staying in tune
as the shadows dogged her blurs and
her slurs as the swingband raced even
raised its tempo-brurs and grurs and
shedo tedo gubba gubbas
a sault and a tumble-weed lightness
as she flung herself right and
down to the floor raised
swiftly to the ceiling
roll roolled and rocck-sockedd into
a rippetyy ripp blues
as the frenzied and the fancied
finger-snapping twos and threes
came out with their maves
singing under their breath about summer
marching in to oh when the saints
oh when the saints come marching in

and love is in the air and
you could hear their hearts beating
as they circled around the girl
now spinning like a machine-drill
boring her way through the stage floor
as she begins her descent
gather wreaths
at the rim of the poem
let it die on your tongue
running out of breath
as it mourns
its own passing

proofread
the lines of your palm
in a gesture of indifference
wide-eyed emptiness

exhausted with its dark labour
giving rise to rumours of fatigue
though it would be hard to verify them
a moon so thin it wilts before the dawn

weep   liquid
grief
                leak
from eyes
damp   walls
peel
                peel
in a heap
                                be ne ath
the window
                struggle
to contain
the gray

slatted   shutters
lament resist
the wind’s
unsolicited keening
bash head
against
wood
                glass
a calibrated lament

hesitant
light   drained
shadow

groping
its way home

with nothing left to lose except
except its silver sheen
the night   waits

at a courteous distance
for us to complete our conversation
in utter silence

will we meet again?
meet perhaps at another removed twilight

I changed dreams stepping back from one and slipping uneasily into another

unhinge the night from its moorings
and let it drift out of sight

its anchor a frayed memory

old shoes with holes etched into soles burnt from too much walking ~~across~~ a landscape tarred with the stale intimacies of aging breath and a bundle of photographs? from a ~~twice~~-lost homeland

[… little did I realize that this image of an imagined migration however forced ~~way back in 1947~~ could be the start of an archive that would house memories of a Partition that split our land into two …]

~~*Death*~~

It could   if it had   thought
of it   in time offered
some consolation

but all it consented to was
a nod of its head   and a brushing back
of an errant lock of hair from
a forehead yet to crease like memory

No one. ~~Not one single person~~. Told me it would be like this. No one. Said
'now remember to straighten your tie and while you are at it polish those shoes and don't forget the lunch box'.
And it is true. I never heard anything like this in my ~~entire~~ life.
I woke up to this grey light on a day that had promised ~~bright~~ sunshine.
Thin layer of dusk. Like dust that clings. Stretching. ~~Across my world~~.
All around me ~~the taps~~. ~~Dripping echoes~~ of hurriedly departing footsteps.
~~Would not~~ stay a second longer.

once laced   with dreams
our conversation
now inhabited
        by pauses

How may I break away from this ‘constrained’ idea of myself as a doer?

Fifty active years have passed in a steadfast refusal to ‘match the numbers’ and I still can’t figure out how to use a calculator.

Somewhere at the periphery sits a shadow with a rainbow upon its head. No rain though.

No desire whatsoever. To visit the land of my forefathers. In any case there is no way in hell anyone will grant a visa.

So much has changed. Not much has remained of those changes. Nothing has changed. Not since Beckett wrote *Godot*.

In Kashmir on way to school. The guilty pleasure of stealing apples from Karan Singh’s orchards. Chased by the maalis.

I carry a thin layer of anxiety under my skin when I travel abroad. Sometimes I can sense it throbbing beneath my pulse. Or is it imagined?

This attachment to the ‘courteous at any cost’ will be my undoing. Maybe.

I failed to learn how to sing in tune. The tune-less-ness has its own attraction. Provided you embrace *outofearshotness*.

why angels   she asked
          I mean why do you write about angels
as in so much about angels   close
my eyes   and I hear
          the sound of wings   I replied
why not bats or flying foxes
she jested
          if its only about the sound of wings flapping   oh
I said
          feeling inadequate   to the occasion and
          the question   thinking deeply
before replying
          perhaps because their wings were not flapping
noisily   merely whispering their distress
          strangled thought half-formed   oh she said
pausing to let the echo settle   also
she began   afresh
                 letting the word hang
                 make itself visible
                 floating before both our eyes
raising my eyebrow
                         and gently shaping my neck   and head
                         and eyes into a question mark
also   she said again
                              only this time plucking it from the air
                              where it levitated   the single word
I notice that you sympathize or
is it the other word   empathize

with the fallen ones
if I may call them that
the angels that are lost
the underdogs of heaven it was true
what she said despite
her slightly ornate way of putting it
or should that be ornamental
you are right I murmured
I hadn't noticed or
at least thought about this
yes she was right I thought to myself
I did tend to ruminate mull chew
a lot more upon the fate of those
once resplendent beings or was it non-beings
that graced the clouds dazzling in the light
of the born again sun
and then for reasons not explicit
or at least not entirely clear
they lost their profound sheen
their proud glitter ruined thus
their wings in tatters
like the aftermath of a sudden storm
storm you asked what storm
and why aftermath of a sudden storm she asked
I had not realized that I had spoken the last few words aloud
as we lay nestling amongst each-other's bodies
feeling the blush of being caught out as it were
creeping across my naked skin
as I struggled to explain the winglessness
of a once angelic body
now merely mortal

UNDER THE SKIN

            … fast forward into a dream
I fail I fail to swipe my screen   I watch it surf my body pink
gold shimmer floating in pink in gold   clouds do
            sunset crawling   my body-naked
            cold wind blowing from the device
alien I no longer recognise
causes the trees growing over the flatlands of my chest to frost over
the low rumble beginning somewhere north of the eyes
up where the forehead cease-merges with the head
my hair no longer jet-black

            I noticed instead a sudden silvering …

            … the sound of a boat
anchoring itself to the wooden pier somewhere close at hand
the crow competing with the blue faced boy's flute …

… a silenced moon wraps itself frantically
into rolls of black and white film
lying at the foot of an old 35 mm projector

            … floating downstream
my dead body on a dirty brown river
strangled by hyacinths with lavender flowers
            mocking its progress
underwater roots conspire   sucking me down
I am alive. I and will any moment right now this very instant
            wake up …

… to a sky slivered into tall green shoots of grass
lazily swaying to the sound of the flute
from that earlier dream
no longer the blue faced boy
but a scarecrow the size of an elephant playing. It trampled the grass
in which I lay unable to stop the dream …

… she sat up all night laying bricks one by one
building a wall while I tried to distract her
inviting her into my dream about a boat long gone into the sun
I followed its silhouetted wake with my eyes shut
I remembered lifting her naked leg
not to disturb the dead snake lying between our sleepless bodies
like a receding afterthought
the blue faced boy sat by my side clutching his flute …

… entering her locked room blindfolded
I heard the flapping of wings
as I hastily unknotted my blindness
the shadows flew from my mother's window
into an indifferent sunlight
I stretched the black fabric across my eyes only to hear the flapping of wings
once again …

… nothing ever moves
in this dream of stillness
not the wind not the trees not the clouds
I am rooted in this landscape my legs buried
in freshly dug earth …

… doors flung apart mangled heap of metal the windshield
a spider web of glass the car crashed my dream as I struggled to shift gears
waking in a room without walls
uprooted trees lay buried in bricks
wounded bleeding over all …

… words lost
crumpled memory of a dream grinding to a halt
the shadows in this dream lengthen
refusing to get caught by the light of the sun
within arm's reach the night gasping …

… he is back   the boy with the flute
the one with the blue face
I see him sitting in the precise spot where the right corner
of the wall
meets the left
he sits whittling away at his flute
as if sharpening a pencil

there will be nothing left …

… through the cracks in the dream the shadows escape
one by one
into a stepwell
down into the still dark brackishness of a dream about drowning …

… the shooting star hurtling into the sea is a dream at daybreak …

… lying on a bed of leaves
hesitating to breathe in case I disturbed the autumn
into stirring …

… a beach hard and silver
the sea a milk pond
foam tickles my feet giddy

rushing
retreating

I bend down to gather the foam
the palms of my hands as sieves …

… a pair of white owls standing outside my window
unmoving unblinking owls drained of blood …

… criss-crossing a room filled with soot in anticipation of a fire
yet to be lit
my footprints searching incessantly for a match …

… neck deep in the dream and sinking further
I heard the crows fly past
noisily …

… crumpled into a white-faced dream
splattered ink …

… the sun collapsing in a heap of shadows
just out of reach the daylight

to wipe the shadows off the wall

… she grabbed the dream from my hands ripped
shredded flung trampled upon the book
sixteen hundred handwritten pages
torn up each

saying

rewrite my life …

… having left the daylight
she hesitated before entering the dream

… the boy with the blue face
swam into the sea making sure to keep the flute dry
the woman rose from the sea naked
her arms tied behind her back with seaweed …

… some dreams
yearn

… in a dream about not being able to write
I bury the white sheets

… before my eyes can adjust to the dream
the night descends as if

… beneath each breath
the protesting murmur of the light

… my feet echoing my unease
I stepped into a street as deserted as your eyes …
… an abandoned alphabet on a sheet of ice
and as cold

… shatter night
into tiny dreams
of daylight chased by shadows

… hovering between my tightly clenched eyelids a grey cloud
curled into a fist refusing to open

… staring at the sun for as long as it takes for the dream to blink

… an entire alphabet of dreams under my feet awaiting trampling

… in this dream I made paper boats

from plain white sheets
to newspapers
to old magazines
to loose pages from torn books
to used envelopes
from countless Christmas cards
deft and capable of staying afloat

and given the right wind
sailing
or speeding
in the momentum generated by rain water
in gutters outside the house
to storms
            by swirling hands
in bathtubs
in this dream
of a thousand paper boats
of different sizes
there is no breeze
nothing can sail
in this stationary landscape
of an entire fleet under siege

I sit continuing to make more boats …

… rushing headlong into the dream
I ended up crashing through to the other side

concussed

my head dizzy with the impact
the dream lying equally shaken all over the floor
I looked in vain

for something in which to gather the shattered pieces
and found instead the blue faced boy
backing off in fear

his flute stretched forward in defense …

… in this room full of blue light
there is not a single face I recognize

there are many faces here
standing shoulder to shoulder
of a similar height
all naked
all bathed in stillness

I can hear them breathing
that's how I know they are alive

that and the way they roll their eyes

all of them in an anti-clock direction
as if to follow with their eyes
            the sound of a distant flute …

            … she gave me a bucket full of soap and water
and a rough grey cloth
as I entered the room
with the seven candles
saying in an abrupt
and commanding tone
that I should proceed to wipe them off the walls

after which
            she pointed in the direction of the restless shadows …

            … responding to the knocking at the door
I hurried to open it
only to see that there was no one there

            … the rain clouds gathered
at the foot of the trees
hanging upside down
            in a room with a painted sky for a floor …

... under the upside down trees
sits the blue faced boy playing his flute
while the clouds that had gathered
in last night's dream begin to fall
the percussive effect
of raindrops
on seared lips ...

... I sat in the furthermost corner of my dream
in the shadow of the slowly revolving fan blades
and watched her lying across the handwritten sentences
of an earlier dream I had inscribed over the white sheet
the bed bending under the weight of my words ...

... trying to open the window and let out the fog
but the window remains jammed
so I take a deep breath

smash my fist through the glass

the fog slowly to bleed ...

… you turn in your sleep
accidentally uncovering your nakedness
the sun embarrassed
murmurs an apology
while I sit
in the furthermost corner of the dream
wondering

why have the fan blades stopped revolving …

… she took the night in her hands
and began to tear it into tiny shreds
after having completed her task she lay down
seemingly to rest and fell into a dreamless sleep …

… in a dream about numbness
the shot of a receding long distance runner
dogged relentless step after step with unflagging rhythm
a heart thumping
towards a horizon running into a sky
made white for …

… eyelids clenched
holding on to a fragile dream …

… speech piled up stacked
these words crammed into space
as tiny or as large
depending on memory
soon the actor will enact speak emote
and language will find utterance
and resonance
only there is no actor
just the dream
meandering amongst the stacks
the words   the imagined utterances
and resonances lost
completely   utterly …

… she kept telling herself
that she must write a monologue
in which the lines lead to dead ends
like wisps of memory forgetting their way home
so you can meander and not be afraid of losing your lines
for they are already lost …

… shatter the calm
as you loudly crumple
crush the sheet toss it into the shadows
flickering on the wall
let rage devour the dream
you have just discarded …

    … I changed dreams
as you would sides
and shovel in hand
    continued to bury the night …

    … the dream emptied of everything
except the fog
surrounding the bed
    with its grey …

    … in stealth
the light entered the room
taking care not to disturb the boy
the one with the blue face
and the now silent flute
as he huddled in the far corner
    dreaming …

    … recede dream depart
take your suitcase with you
the one I had packed long ago
with neatly folded shadows
smoothened with the palm of my hand
nothing will be left behind
    in this house with the peeling walls …

… inhabit the dream
the one at the end of the line
patiently waiting
to come out of the shadow …

… I dream of the future
the one that lies in tatters somewhere
behind me …

… multiple mourners mourning
their own deaths silhouetted
against a darkening horizon
shadows created by puppets …

… in whispers
from an exhausted defeated throat
a past that continues to haunt dreams

remembering …

… the sound of stammering
dreams in the wind
or brightly coloured flags
atop a mountain or
perhaps a heath a
high flat piece of land
one that is visited
by winds without mercy
not cruel just lacking
in sensitivity…

… eyes
tight fists
in motion

blurred

images
of a vision made dream
landscapes
gathered
over seasons
one merging into another
refuse to settle
a sleeping wakefulness …

… eyelids slammed
shut
like a prison cell
just out of reach
the waking up
trapped as it were
in a dream
its edges tinted by a dawn

THREE POEMS

Pascal Q
From the very first
B Rush-stroke
bccafeghrkteatime under the rock

whEn A lice without the A lice

set out to infestinfectcrawlallover the body of a polity
an entire citizen wrY uptoits Neck in what
can only be de——scribed as The Plague

~~And they stand opposed as two poles.~~
~~In active predation, in the springing of carnivores~~
~~as they leap on their prey—in the projection of all those~~
~~beings projecting themselves onto their opposite pole~~
~~the background and~~ the admirable body that moves and
stands out against it are suddenly uncoupled.

Hunting is ~~the background of art~~.

Lying in wait ~~the background of contemplation~~.

Hunger ~~the background of desire~~.

Carnivorousness ~~the background of admiration~~.

Time ~~was first conceived as~~ predation. Beings as
Its prey.

4 red capsicums 2 yellow capsicums 1 green Zuchini 1 small iceberg lettuce 100 grms rocket leaves 2 heads romaine lettuce 100 grms snow peas 200 grms cherry tomato 2 bok choy 2 packets mushrooms 1 avocado 50 grms parsley 50 grms basil 1 leek 100 grms baby carrots 100 grms baby corn 1 small red cabbage 1 kg large potatoes 1 kg small potatoes 2 beetroots 1 kg large baigan 1/2 kg small baigan 1 kg taroi 1/2 kg Bhindi 1 small lauki 2 bundles Palak 300 grms pumpkin 1 small cabbage 1/2 kg kundru 1/2 kg laU saag 3 capsicum 1 bundle Lal saag 1 bundle kalmi saag 200 grms Dhania patta 100 grms pudina patta 1 kaccha Aam 12 nimbus Green chillies 1 watermelon

between the red of the capsicum and the red of the exploding watermelon all that remains of the shopping list is an empty plastic shopping bag

jesus

there are no nails, though, nor the sound of shuffling feet, or angels wings that flapped in anxiety, no. just this imagined weight of a cross you once bore
jesus

as you speed-walk, the thorns bleed their hearts out, and the lips that have never known thirst, thirst
jesus

your eyes pasted steadfast on the earth, as you bend under the weight of shadows you once cast out

the wind is no match for the brisk pace you set as you carry your own cross

amen

Knotted Grief
by Naveen Kishore

First published 2022

POETRY

ISBN: 978-0-6451030-7-6

BOOK, TYPESETTING, AND LOGO DESIGN
Mountains Brown Press

PUBLISHER
Life Before Man

Gazebo Books
PO Box 375
Summer Hill
New South Wales 2130
Australia

gazebobooks.com.au

COVER IMAGE: *Chamber*, 2021, oil on canvas, 240 x 92 cm, © Phil Day

www.ingramcontent.com/pod-product-compliance
Lightning Source LLC
LaVergne TN
LVHW051006080826
845145LV00009B/2492

* 9 7 8 0 6 4 5 1 0 3 0 7 6 *